Spring Harvest
Bible Workbook

TRUST

Enduring hope

Eric Gaudion

Series editor for thematic workbooks – Jeff Lucas

Authentic

SPRING HARVEST

Equipping the Church for action

12 11 10 09 08 07 06 7 6 5 4 3 2 1

First published in 2006 by Spring Harvest Publishing Division and Authentic Media
9 Holdom Avenue, Bletchley, Milton Keynes, Bucks, MK1 1QR, UK
and 129 Mobilization Drive, Waynesboro, GA 30830-4575, USA

www.authenticmedia.co.uk

Authentic Media is a division of Send the Light Ltd, a company limited by guarantee
(registered charity no. 270162)

British Library Cataloguing in Publication Data

A catalogue record for this book is available from the British Library

ISBN 1-85078-686-0

Typeset by Spring Harvest
Cover design by fourninezero design
Print management by Adare Carwin
Printed and Bound by J. H. Haynes & Co. Ltd., Sparkford

CONTENTS

ABOUT THIS BOOK

This study book gets behind the scenes of the lives of people in the Bible who trusted God despite desperate circumstances. Their struggles with believing in the middle of intense personal suffering encourage us to keep on trusting and hoping. We will also investigate answers to the questions raised by suffering and pain.

This workbook is written primarily for use in a group situation, but can easily be used by individuals who want to study the biblical picture of God. It can be used in a variety of contexts, so it is perhaps helpful to spell out the assumptions that we have made about the groups that will use it. These can have a variety of names – home groups, Bible study groups, cell groups – we've used housegroup as the generic term.

▶ The emphasis of the studies will be on the application of the Bible. Group members will not just learn facts, but will be encouraged to think: 'How does this apply to me? What change does it require of me? What incidents or situations in my life is this relevant to?'
▶ Housegroups can encourage honesty and make space for questions and doubts. The aim of the studies is not to find the 'right answer', but to help members understand the Bible by working through the questions. The Christian faith throws up paradoxes. Events in people's lives may make particular verses difficult to understand. The housegroup should be a safe place to express these concerns.
▶ Housegroups can give opportunities for deep friendships to develop. Group members will be encouraged to talk about their experiences, feelings, questions, hopes and fears. They will be able to offer one another pastoral support and to get involved in each other's lives.
▶ There is a difference between being a collection of individuals who happen to meet together every Wednesday and being an effective group who bounce ideas off each other, spark inspiration and creativity and pool their talents and resources to create solutions together and whose whole is definitely greater than the sum of its parts. The process of working through these studies will encourage healthy group dynamics.

Space is given for you to write answers, comments, questions and thoughts. This book will not tell you what to think, but will help you to discover the truth of God's word through thinking, discussing, praying and listening.

FOR GROUP MEMBERS

▶ You will get more out of the study if you spend some time during the week reading the passage and thinking about the questions. Make a note of anything you don't understand.

▶ Pray that God will help you to understand the passage and show you how to apply it. Pray for other members in the group too, that they will find the study helpful.

▶ Be willing to take part in the discussions. The leader of the group is not there as an expert with all the answers. They will want everyone to get involved and share their thoughts and opinions.

▶ However, don't dominate the group! If you are aware that you are saying a lot, make space for others to contribute. Be sensitive to other group members and aim to be encouraging. If you disagree with someone, say so but without putting down their contribution.

FOR INDIVIDUALS

▶ Although this book is written with a group in mind, it can also be easily used by individuals. You obviously won't be able to do the group activities suggested, but you can consider how you would answer the questions and write your thoughts in the space provided.

▶ You may find it helpful to talk to a prayer partner about what you have learnt, and ask them to pray for you as you try and apply what you are learning to your life.

▶ The New International Version of the text is printed in the book. If you usually use a different version, then read from your own Bible as well.

INTRODUCTION

INTRODUCTION

There are differing kinds of faith and different levels of God's active intervention in our lives. The apparent inaction of God in our circumstances may possibly signal a need for growth and the deepening of our faith. Certainly there are times in our Christian walk when God appears to be silent or far away and we feel as though we are on our own. If you are familiar with the poem *Footprints in the sand* you will know that these are just the times when God is closest to us, and even carrying us.

There is a kind of faith, however, that we need in order to keep on believing and trusting when life is hard and there is no obvious sign of the Lord's presence. It is the faith that perseveres. Such faith may seem difficult to sustain, but there are very special resources in the Bible to help us to do so. God gives the Holy Spirit also to those who simply hang in there and trust when everything seems to be going in the opposite direction to their expectations and desires.

This kind of faith can only develop and grow through increasing pressure and prolonged hardship. It proves its presence not by receiving a miracle, but by receiving instead the courage and trust to go through, instead of come out of, trials. Some of the world's most precious commodities are found in the deepest, darkest places. Diamonds, gold, silver, precious stones, uranium and coal are all mined by people working with great effort, at supreme risk and sometimes at great depth. So are the benefits of trust and enduring hope. They come as a fulfilment of God's promise 'I will give you the treasures of darkness, riches stored in secret places, so that you may know that I am the LORD, the God of Israel, who summons you by name' (Is. 45:3).

In this workbook we will follow Joseph through betrayal by his family and into jail in a foreign land. The story of Gideon will help us to examine our sense of worth, while Job's sufferings will inspire and encourage us to worship despite our trials. The New Testament offers us assistance in our journey towards trust and enduring hope by allowing us to look behind the scenes at the trust of Simon Peter that enabled him to defy gravity and take a great step of faith, despite being terrified. Paul also suffered much and we will discover how he trusted when facing possible death by drowning in an appalling storm. He also knew what it was to plead earnestly with God to remove a thorn in his flesh and have that prayer refused. Both Romans 8 and Hebrews 11 offer helpful insights into the way that we should trust, no matter what may be going wrong in our lives.

In all this we can do no better than look at the example of Jesus. He trusted his Heavenly Father right through Gethsemane and Calvary, and rose again from the dead to offer us his power to keep on trusting.

TRUST WHEN REJECTED

Aim: to see how Joseph trusted despite being rejected and imprisoned

TO SET THE SCENE

Things are not always as they first appear to be!

A young man, badly injured in a car accident, has been brought into a hospital's accident and emergency department. The doctor determines that emergency brain surgery is required. Accordingly, the brain surgeon is paged. Upon seeing the patient, the surgeon exclaims, 'My God, I can't operate on that boy! He's my son!'

That is so, but the surgeon is not the boy's father. Who is the surgeon?

Read the passage together

Now his brothers had gone to graze their father's flocks near Shechem, and Israel said to Joseph, "As you know, your brothers are grazing the flocks near Shechem. Come, I am going to send you to them." "Very well," he replied. So he said to him, "Go and see if all is well with your brothers and with the flocks, and bring word back to me." Then he sent him off from the Valley of Hebron. When Joseph arrived at Shechem, a man found him wandering around in the fields and asked him, "What are you looking for?" He replied, "I'm looking for my brothers. Can you tell me where they are grazing their flocks?"

"They have moved on from here," the man answered. "I heard them say, 'Let's go to Dothan.'" "So Joseph went after his brothers and found them near Dothan. But they saw him in the distance, and before he reached them, they plotted to kill him.

"Here comes that dreamer!" they said to each other. "Come now, let's kill him and throw him into one of these cisterns and say that a ferocious animal devoured him. Then we'll see what comes of his dreams." When Reuben heard this, he tried to rescue him from their hands. "Let's not take his life," he said. "Don't shed any blood. Throw him into this cistern here in the desert, but don't

lay a hand on him." Reuben said this to rescue him from them and take him back to his father.

So when Joseph came to his brothers, they stripped him of his robe—the richly ornamented robe he was wearing—and they took him and threw him into the cistern. Now the cistern was empty; there was no water in it. As they sat down to eat their meal, they looked up and saw a caravan of Ishmaelites coming from Gilead. Their camels were loaded with spices, balm and myrrh, and they were on their way to take them down to Egypt.

Judah said to his brothers, "What will we gain if we kill our brother and cover up his blood? Come, let's sell him to the Ishmaelites and not lay our hands on him; after all, he is our brother, our own flesh and blood." His brothers agreed. So when the Midianite merchants came by, his brothers pulled Joseph up out of the cistern and sold him for twenty shekels of silver to the Ishmaelites, who took him to Egypt. When Reuben returned to the cistern and saw that Joseph was not there, he tore his clothes. He went back to his brothers and said, "The boy isn't there! Where can I turn now?"

Then they got Joseph's robe, slaughtered a goat and dipped the robe in the blood. They took the ornamented robe back to their father and said, "We found this. Examine it to see whether it is your son's robe." He recognized it and said, "It is my son's robe! Some ferocious animal has devoured him. Joseph has surely been torn to pieces."

Then Jacob tore his clothes, put on sackcloth and mourned for his son many days. All his sons and daughters came to comfort him, but he refused to be comforted. "No," he said, "in mourning will I go down to the grave to my son." So his father wept for him.

Meanwhile, the Midianites sold Joseph in Egypt to Potiphar, one of Pharaoh's officials, the captain of the guard.

Genesis 37:12–36

JOSEPH'S STORY

Joseph spent time in jail because of his brothers' rejection. He suffered years of torment due to their hatred. One day the chance came to pay them back. He was then the new Prime Minister of Egypt, and they came before him cap in hand to ask for famine relief. Instead of seeking revenge, Joseph's attitude was remarkable, because he was trusting God.

1. Look at Genesis 37:1–11 and list why Joseph's brothers treated him in the way they did. How do you think Joseph should have dealt with his dreams and their possible interpretations?

WHAT DOES
SEARCH
THE BIBLE SAY?

2. Read verses 21–22 and Genesis 42:21–22. What was Reuben's reaction to the decision to kill or sell Joseph? Why did he react in this way?

WHAT DOES
SEARCH
THE BIBLE SAY?

3. Take a look at Genesis 39:1–6a. Things initially went well for Joseph in Egypt. Why?

4. Even when Joseph landed up in jail because of a false allegation of attempted rape, he still seemed to be trusting God (Gen. 39:20–23 and 40:8). How do we know this?

ENGAGING WITH
THE WORLD

5. What impact do you think Joseph's attitude would have had on his jailors and fellow-prisoners? Would those who know you (especially those outside the faith community) be as confident about your trustworthiness and competence?

HOW DOES THIS
?
APPLY TO ME

6. How would you feel in Joseph's situation? Have you experienced rejection by close colleagues, family or friends? How did you cope?

7. When the time came for the guilty brothers to stand before Joseph and plead for his help, he said these remarkable words: 'So then, it was not you who sent me here, but God' (Gen. 45:8). What had brought Joseph to that conclusion?

8. Look at Genesis 50:18–21. When Jacob died, Joseph's brothers expected retaliation for their betrayal. What did they get instead? What shows that Joseph had forgiven them completely?

HOW DOES THIS APPLY TO ME

9. Are there people in your past who need that reaction from you?

WORSHIP
Read Psalm 62:1-8.
Picture the face of someone who has rejected or lied about you in the past. Ask God to give you the grace to forgive them. Pray for God's blessing in their lives.

Listen to *Only You* by Andy Park.

DURING THE WEEK
Pray for those who have betrayed or rejected you. Ask God to help you show the kind of attitude towards them that Joseph did towards his brothers. Pray for the strength to keep trusting God and other people despite your experiences in the past.

FOR FURTHER STUDY
Read the whole story of Joseph from Genesis 37 to 50, and look for further evidence of his steadfast trust in God despite all his troubles. For an excellent commentary on the story of Joseph, see RT Kendall's *God meant it for good*.[1]

---

1 RT Kendall, *God meant it for good*, (Carlisle: Authentic, 2003)

TRUST VERSUS SELF-DOUBT

Aim: to see how Gideon trusted despite his self-doubt

Read the passage together

The angel of the LORD came and sat down under the oak in Ophrah that belonged to Joash the Abiezrite, where his son Gideon was threshing wheat in a winepress to keep it from the Midianites. When the angel of the LORD appeared to Gideon, he said, "The LORD is with you, mighty warrior."

"But sir," Gideon replied, "if the LORD is with us, why has all this happened to us? Where are all his wonders that our fathers told us about when they said, 'Did not the LORD bring us up out of Egypt?' But now the LORD has abandoned us and put us into the hand of Midian."

The LORD turned to him and said, "Go in the strength you have and save Israel out of Midian's hand. Am I not sending you?"

"But Lord," Gideon asked, "how can I save Israel? My clan is the weakest in Manasseh, and I am the least in my family."

The LORD answered, "I will be with you, and you will strike down all the Midianites together."

Gideon replied, "If now I have found favour in your eyes, give me a sign that it is really you talking to me. Please do not go away until I come back and bring my offering and set it before you."

And the LORD said, "I will wait until you return."

Gideon went in, prepared a young goat, and from an ephah of flour he made bread without yeast. Putting the meat in a basket and its broth in a pot, he brought them out and offered them to him under the oak.

The angel of God said to him, "Take the meat and the unleavened bread, place them on this rock, and pour out the broth." And Gideon did so. With the tip of the staff that was in his hand, the angel of the Lord touched the meat and the unleavened bread. Fire flared from the rock, consuming the meat and the bread. And the angel of the Lord disappeared. When Gideon realised that it was the angel of the Lord, he exclaimed, "Ah, Sovereign Lord! I have seen the angel of the Lord face to face!"

But the Lord said to him, "Peace! Do not be afraid. You are not going to die."

So Gideon built an altar to the Lord there and called it The Lord is Peace. To this day it stands in Ophrah of the Abiezrites.

That same night the Lord said to him, "Take the second bull from your father's herd, the one seven years old. Tear down your father's altar to Baal and cut down the Asherah pole beside it. Then build a proper kind of altar to the Lord your God on the top of this height. Using the wood of the Asherah pole that you cut down, offer the second bull as a burnt offering."

So Gideon took ten of his servants and did as the Lord told him. But because he was afraid of his family and the men of the town, he did it at night rather than in the daytime. In the morning when the men of the town got up, there was Baal's altar, demolished, with the Asherah pole beside it cut down and the second bull sacrificed on the newly-built altar! They asked each other, "Who did this?" When they carefully investigated, they were told, "Gideon son of Joash did it."

Gideon said to God, "If you will save Israel by my hand as you have promised— look, I will place a wool fleece on the threshing-floor. If there is dew only on the fleece and all the ground is dry, then I will know that you will save Israel by my hand, as you said." And that is what happened. Gideon rose early the next day; he squeezed the fleece and wrung out the dew—a bowlful of water. Then Gideon said to God, "Do not be angry with me. Let me make just one more request. Allow me one more test with the fleece. This time make the fleece dry and the ground covered with dew." That night God did so. Only the fleece was dry; all the ground was covered with dew.

Judges 6:11−29, 36−40

ABOUT JUDGES AND GIDEON

The book of Judges is a catalogue of the consequences faced when God's covenant people forget him. There is a cycle that repeats itself throughout Judges.

- Sin in the hearts and practices of the people.
- The oppression of Israel by one or more of her national neighbours as an expression of God's wrath (Judg. 2:14).
- The Israelites repent and call upon the Lord for mercy.
- God sends a deliverer to lead his people out of oppression and invasion (Judg. 2:16). The people that God chose to be judges and to lead Israel to victory were not champions of justice, experts in military strategy, or with exceptional abilities to lead others and suppress national enemies. They were ordinary Israelites called and equipped for a specific task. Gideon was one of these.

The Midianites were nomads who made long-distance raids on their neighbours. They arrived in Israel every spring, pitching their tents in Canaan, on the hills and fields of the farming areas, leaving again each winter. There was conflict between them and the inhabitants of the land, whom they virtually enslaved. Gideon was one in a long line of 'judges' who fought these invaders. He began with the religious reform of his own family, and then the nation, followed by military action guided by God.

TO SET THE SCENE

Gideon was surprised by the greeting of the angel. Surprise members of your group by highlighting some strong point or some potential that you recognise in them (even if they don't)! Make sure it is positive: 'Eileen, you're a real encourager', 'John, you're a great driver', 'Fred, you've got a real servant heart', and so on. Write these down on slips of paper, one per person.

Gideon felt that he was the last person God might choose to throw out the enemy forces from Israel and lead a nationwide religious revival, yet God saw the potential in him. When called by the Lord, Gideon chose to trust in God's word rather than his own feelings of worthlessness and fear.

WHAT DOES **SEARCH** **THE BIBLE SAY?** **1.** Read Judges 6:1–6. What impact were the frequent invasions of Israel by the nomadic Midianites having upon the farming communities in particular?

WHAT DOES **SEARCH** **THE BIBLE SAY?** **2.** Where did the angel appear to Gideon, and what does this venue tell us about his state of mind? What was Gideon's reaction to the salutation of the angel (vv 12–13)?

3. Compare the salutation of the angel to Gideon with that given to Mary in Luke 1:28 and her reaction in verse 29. What does this say to you regarding the way God felt about these individuals and the way they felt about themselves?

4. Look at Gideon's argument with the angel in verses 13–14. Upon what evidence did Gideon base his claim that God had abandoned Israel? Was he right?

5. When Gideon realised that his complaint had been over-ruled and that he was still being given this call of God, he argued that he was unfit for duty. On what basis (v 15)?

6. How did God respond to his plea? Compare this with the way God responded to a similar argument from Moses in Exodus 3:10–12a. What similarities are there?

HOW DOES THIS **APPLY TO ME** **7.** Does the way God feels about you, as revealed in the Bible, differ from how you feel about yourself? Which should we take to be the truth – our feelings or God's revelation? Have you ever been asked to do something for God and been reluctant because you felt you or your family were not up to it?

8. Judges 6:17–24 shows that Gideon became aware that he had met with God. What did he do when he realised this?

9. What do you feel about Gideon's request for a sign in verses 36–40? Does this show trust in God, or the opposite? Is this showing us the way that we should seek divine guidance today?

WORSHIP
Read out loud some scriptures that tell of God's love towards us, and focus on his revelation rather than your own sense of worth. Gideon's trust was shown in his willingness to obey despite his fear and his low sense of self-esteem. Listen to the song *Have your way in me*. Pray that God will have his way in your life, despite the way you may feel about yourself right now.

DURING THE WEEK
Here is an activity for you try this week.

Complete the test opposite then compare your score with the comments below.

Total score	Comments
56–60:	Either you have an excellent self-esteem, or you see yourself more highly than you should, or you faked the test!
46–55:	You seem to have a high estimation of yourself and should have few problems with self-esteem.
36–45:	Your overall score is neither high or low. There may be specific areas where you scored low and which need attention.
Below 35:	If you answered the test honestly, you have a real need for improvement in how you see yourself.

Note
If you scored low, and feel this is a true reflection of how you feel about yourself, you might find it helpful to talk with a trusted Christian friend or counsellor. Consider the particular questions on which you scored low, as this may indicate in which particular aspects of self-esteem you need help with.

FOR FURTHER STUDY
Look at the way that the people whom God called for his service in the Bible were only too well aware of their own shortcomings, yet trusted in God's word rather than in their feelings.

Isaiah 6:1–8: the call of Isaiah. Notice verses 5-8 in particular.

Jeremiah 1:4–8: God calls Jeremiah to speak for him.

Luke 5:1–11: Jesus calls Simon Peter into ministry, despite Simon's protests.

ACTIVITY: SELF-ESTEEM MEASURE[2]

This little test will help you get a better idea of how you see yourself. Answer as honestly as you can. Rate yourself on each question using this system:

Definitely or almost always: 3
Probably or often: 2
Probably not or seldom: 1
Definitely not or almost never: 0

Self-esteem measure

1. I am truly content with the way I look.
2. I feel positive about facing new challenges.
3. I consider my ability to think and reason adequate.
4. I think people enjoy being with me.
5. I am satisfied with the degree of success I'm experiencing so far in my life.
6. I feel as worthwhile when I'm just having a good time as when I'm doing something constructive.
7. I consistently forgive myself when I make mistakes.
8. When I make a mistake I refrain from telling myself negative things (such as: 'I'm stupid, clumsy, can't do anything right, etc').
9. I can honestly say that I love myself.
10. Deep down, I feel that God accepts me just the way I am.
11. When I look at myself in the mirror, I'm happy with what I see.
12. I feel competent to tackle most new jobs.
13. I am genuinely happy with my intellectual ability.
14. I feel good about my personality.
15. Overall, I regard myself as successful in life.
16. I feel of great value and worth to God, even when I fail.
17. When I do something wrong or unwise I quickly get over being angry with myself.
18. My thoughts towards myself are usually positive, rather than critical.
19. I appreciate myself, even though I'm not perfect.
20. Though I realise I'm a sinner, deep down I can truly feel that God sees me as holy and blameless through Christ.

TOTAL
Self-esteem total score

2 Taken from *Teamwork*, copyright ©2003 Gordon and Rosemary Jones, published by Scripture Union and used with permission.

TRUST UNDER ATTACK

AIM

Aim: to see how Job's trust enabled him to worship

TO SET THE SCENE

Listen to the CD track *Come now is the time to worship.*

ABOUT THE BOOK OF JOB

The book of Job deserves a far deeper treatment than can be given in one study. In it we see the death of the self-life through the fires of affliction and the direct revelation of God. Job is a very early piece of literature. Job himself may well have been a contemporary of the Patriarchs, even though the book could have been written later. Yet, despite its antiquity, Job is rightly described by Gordon Fee as 'true wisdom at its finest'. At the core of the book is the meaning of suffering which Job wrestles with. How can we reconcile God's holiness and the existence of evil? Are the kingdoms of good and evil two opposite but equal domains? Does sin lead to suffering or does God allow pain and difficulties in order to fulfil his good purposes for his people?

Job is, in many ways, representative of all believers, in that trusting in the midst of suffering is a challenge common to being human.

Read the passage together

> On another day the angels came to present themselves before the LORD, and Satan also came with them to present himself before him. And the LORD said to Satan, "Where have you come from?"
>
> Satan answered the LORD, "From roaming through the earth and going to and fro in it."
>
> Then the LORD said to Satan, "Have you considered my servant Job? There is no-one on earth like him; he is blameless and upright, a man who fears God and shuns evil. And he still maintains his integrity, though you incited me against him to ruin him without any reason."

"Skin for skin!" Satan replied. "A man will give all he has for his own life. But stretch out your hand and strike his flesh and bones, and he will surely curse you to your face."

The LORD said to Satan, "Very well, then, he is in your hands; but you must spare his life."

So Satan went out from the presence of the LORD and afflicted Job with painful sores from the soles of his feet to the top of his head. Then Job took a piece of broken pottery and scraped himself with it as he sat among the ashes. His wife said to him, "Are you still holding on to your integrity? Curse God and die!"

He replied, "You are talking like a foolish woman. Shall we accept good from God, and not trouble?" In all this, Job did not sin in what he said.

Job 2:1–10

If Job is one of the oldest books in the Bible, then the faith that Job showed in God and his redeeming love was before its time. It is even more remarkable when you consider the terrible tests Satan put him through.

WHAT DOES
SEARCH
THE BIBLE SAY?

1. Look at Job 1:2–3, 13–19 and list the various tragedies that occurred in Job's household.

2. In chapter 2 the trial is extended to include Job's health. Satan was convinced that if Job's body was afflicted he would curse God. What kept Job from doing so (see 1:5, 9–10)?

3. Some might claim (like Job's friends) that sin automatically leads to God's wrath and to suffering, but what does verse 3 tell us about God's attitude towards Job?

4. What does the glimpse behind the scenes of eternity in verses 6–12 tell you about the part played by Satan in Job's life? Does this add anything to the way that you already think of the devil?

5. How do you feel about Job's statement in verse 10, 'Shall we accept good from God, and not trouble' as it relates to your own life?

'We frequently find ourselves, instead of acting as we had planned, reacting to an unexpected turn of events. We make plans but are often forced to change those plans. But our unexpected change of plan is part of God's plan. God is never surprised; never caught off guard; never frustrated by unexpected developments. God does as he pleases and that which pleases him is always for his glory and our good.'[3]

6. Read Job 19:23–27. What was remarkable about the kind of trust that Job expresses here? How do you think it helped him through his illness, loss and the criticism of his friends?

7. Read Job 23:10–12. According to verse 10, how did Job regard his troubles? What aspect of Job's trust in God is revealed in verse 11? What resource for his trust does Job reveal in verse 12?

8. Job was criticised by those who should have been his main supporters – his wife and his friends. How good is the community of faith around you at supporting those facing harsh trials of different kinds? What more could be done?

9. In Job 1:20–21 Job worshipped God despite his great loss. How do you think he managed to do that?

10. Can you think of times when you have been in real difficulties, yet have chosen to worship God despite your feelings? How did things work out?

'Caught up amidst a whirlwind of pain and confusion, the decision to cry out "Yet I will praise You" is a costly act of devotion. In the life of every worshipper there will come times when worship meets with suffering. And these moments shape what kind of worshippers we will become.'[4]

WORSHIP

Read Habakkuk 3:17–19. Spend a few moments rejoicing in the Lord and thanking God for who he is, despite the changing circumstances of our lives. Pray for those members of the group who feel that they can really identify with Job, or with Habakkuk's list of woes.

DURING THE WEEK

Look at Job 3:11–13 and see how Job's friends started out to help Job in quite an effective way – identifying with him silently in his suffering. Ask the Lord to help you to be an effective friend to someone in real trouble. Plan to write to someone or send a card to encourage them. Share with the group your plan as a commitment, so that they can check with you next week that you have been successful.

FOR FURTHER STUDY

Read Job chapters 4 and 5. The speech of Eliphaz sounds so plausible. Now that you know what happened in chapters 1 and 2, see if you can detect the faults in what Job's friend is saying. You could repeat the exercise for each of the friends: Eliphaz, Bildad and Zophar.

Read Job chapters 38–42 and observe what the Lord said in response to the accusations made by the friends of Job. See also the final end of Job in 42:7–16.

3 Jerry Bridges *Trusting God* (Colorado Springs: Navpress, 1991) p47–48
4 Matt and Beth Redman, *Blessed be Your Name* (London: Hodder and Stoughton, 2005) 19–20.

TRUST WHEN TERRIFIED

Aim: to see how trust led Peter to take an enormous risk

TO SET THE SCENE

Ask group members to divide up into twos and tell one another their most terrifying experience. Did faith play any part in this experience? If not, would you approach it in a different way now?

Read the passage together

Immediately Jesus made the disciples get into the boat and go on ahead of him to the other side, while he dismissed the crowd. After he had dismissed them, he went up on a mountainside by himself to pray. When evening came, he was there alone, but the boat was already a considerable distance from land, buffeted by the waves because the wind was against it.

During the fourth watch of the night Jesus went out to them, walking on the lake.

When the disciples saw him walking on the lake, they were terrified. "It's a ghost," they said, and cried out in fear. But Jesus immediately said to them: "Take courage! It is I. Don't be afraid."

"Lord, if it's you," Peter replied, "tell me to come to you on the water."

"Come," he said. Then Peter got down out of the boat, walked on the water and came towards Jesus. But when he saw the wind, he was afraid and, beginning to sink, cried out, "Lord, save me!"

Immediately Jesus reached out his hand and caught him. "You of little faith," he said, "why did you doubt?" And when they climbed into the boat, the wind died down.

Then those who were in the boat worshipped him, saying, "Truly you are the Son of God."

Matthew 14:22–33

Jesus gave his disciples instructions to get into a boat and cross to the other side of the lake. They were probably surprised to encounter such strong opposing winds, and must have found the journey hard. What they certainly did not expect was to see Jesus – and then one of their own number – walking on the water. This was a real crash course in trust.

1. Why were the disciples on the Sea of Galilee at night and without Jesus? Where did Jesus go when they set off and why?

WHAT DOES
SEARCH
THE BIBLE SAY?

2. Look at Mark 6:47–48 and John 6:19. What do these verses tell you about the attitude of Jesus towards his disciples while he was up the mountainside praying?

3. According to verse 26, what emotion did the disciples experience when they saw the Lord? How did Jesus address the disciples in verse 27 and what does that tell you about what God wants us to do when we're afraid?

HOW DOES THIS
?
APPLY TO ME

4. Have you seen God working in extra-ordinary or even scary ways? How did you cope?

WHAT DOES
SEARCH
THE BIBLE SAY?

5. Three of the gospels tell of Jesus walking on the water (see also Mk. 6:45–51 and Jn. 6:15–21) but only Matthew reports Peter going over the side to Jesus. Why is this missing, even from the account in Mark that may have been dictated by Peter himself?

6. Getting out of the boat in a storm must have been a tremendous risk. John Ortberg has said that if you want to walk on the water you have got to get out of the boat.[5] Upon what evidence did Peter base his step of faith?

5 John Ortberg, *If you want to walk on water you have got to get out of the boat* (Grand Rapids: Zondervan, 2001)

When Luciano Pavarotti was a boy, his grandmother often put him on her lap and said, 'You're going to be great, you'll see.' His grandmother, however, had dreams of Luciano becoming a banker! Instead, he became a school teacher. He taught elementary school for a while, singing infrequently at special events. His father was the one who goaded him into developing his voice, chiding him for singing below his potential. Finally, at age twenty-two, Pavarotti stopped teaching to sell insurance. He continued to look for something financially stable to rely on, in case he couldn't make it in the music world. However, the insurance business allowed him time to take voice lessons, and the rest is history. The opera star now says, 'Studying voice was the turning point of my life. It's a mistake to take the safe path in life.' He adds with a twinkle in his eye, 'My teacher groomed me. But no teacher ever told me I would become famous. Just my grandmother.'

It takes courage to leave a position you consider safe and launch out in a new direction. But without taking a risk, you can never realise your potential or know all God created you to be.

7. Martin Luther defined faith as 'a living, daring confidence in God's grace.' When was the last time your church took a daring step of faith that involved risk? What about you? Is there some step of faith that you feel God is calling you to take now or in the future?

8. Why did Peter begin to sink? How did he react when he realised that he was going down?

9. Why do you think that Jesus rebuked Peter, given that Peter trusted enough to get out of the boat in the first place?

10. The picture of Jesus and Peter walking back to the boat together, hand in hand, treading on the very sea that was threatening to engulf them all, must have astounded the other disciples. What made the difference in Peter's attitude that enabled him to do this?

WORSHIP

Take a moment to consider whether God may be calling you to trust him enough to take a significant step of faith, even if it involves risk. Pray for one another as you set out to be obedient to God this week, whatever the risks involved. Read Luke 1:26–38. Look at verses 37–38 and consider the statement of the angel and Mary's response. Pray that our responses to God's challenges will be equally trusting.

DURING THE WEEK

Ask the Lord each day to show you if there is some step of faith you need to take. Pray for those in the group who shared that there is a step of faith they need to take. Give them a call and see how they are getting on.

When you are afraid, pray that the Lord's presence will become clear to you in spite of the frightening circumstances. Look at some of the other times that Jesus tells his followers not to be afraid (Mt. 17:7, 28:8–10; Acts 18:9–10, Rev. 1:17–18). Perhaps it would be good to phone your group leader or a trusted friend to share this fear with them for prayer?

FOR FURTHER STUDY

In preparation for next week's study, look at some other situations in the Bible where God used storms to speak very clearly to his followers: Job 38:1, 40:6–9, Jonah 1 and Matthew 8:23–27.

TRUST WHEN ALL HOPE IS GONE

Aim: to see how Paul trusted when faced with possible death

Read the passage together

Much time had been lost, and sailing had already become dangerous because by now it was after the Fast. So Paul warned them, "Men, I can see that our voyage is going to be disastrous and bring great loss to ship and cargo, and to our own lives also." But the centurion, instead of listening to what Paul said, followed the advice of the pilot and of the owner of the ship. Since the harbour was unsuitable to winter in, the majority decided that we should sail on, hoping to reach Phoenix and winter there. This was a harbour in Crete, facing both south-west and north-west.

When a gentle south wind began to blow, they thought they had obtained what they wanted; so they weighed anchor and sailed along the shore of Crete. Before very long, a wind of hurricane force, called the "north-easter," swept down from the island. The ship was caught by the storm and could not head into the wind; so we gave way to it and were driven along. As we passed to the lee of a small island called Cauda, we were hardly able to make the lifeboat secure. When the men had hoisted it aboard, they passed ropes under the ship itself to hold it together. Fearing that they would run aground on the sand-bars of Syrtis, they lowered the sea anchor and let the ship be driven along. We took such a violent battering from the storm that the next day they began to throw the cargo overboard. On the third day, they threw the ship's tackle overboard with their own hands. When neither sun nor stars appeared for many days and the storm continued raging, we finally gave up all hope of being saved.

After the men had gone a long time without food, Paul stood up before them and said: "Men, you should have taken my advice not to sail from Crete; then you would have spared yourselves this damage and loss. But now I urge you to keep up your courage, because not one of you will be lost; only the ship will be destroyed. Last night an angel of the God whose I am and whom I serve stood beside mean and said, 'Do not be afraid, Paul. You must stand trial before Caesar; and God has graciously given you the lives of all who sail with you.' So keep up your courage, men, for I have faith in God that it will happen just as he told me. Nevertheless, we must run aground on some island."

On the fourteenth night we were still being driven across the Adriatic Sea, when about midnight the sailors sensed they were approaching land. They took soundings and found that the water was one hundred and twenty feet deep. A short time later they took soundings again and found it was ninety feet deep. Fearing that we would be dashed against the rocks, they dropped four anchors from the stern and prayed for daylight. In an attempt to escape from the ship, the sailors let the lifeboat down into the sea, pretending they were going to lower some anchors from the bow. Then Paul said to the centurion and the soldiers, "Unless these men stay with the ship, you cannot be saved." So the soldiers cut the ropes that held the lifeboat and let it fall away.

Just before dawn Paul urged them all to eat. "For the last fourteen days," he said, "you have been in constant suspense and have gone without food—you haven't eaten anything. Now I urge you to take some food. You need it to survive. Not one of you will lose a single hair from his head." After he said this, he took some bread and gave thanks to God in front of them all. Then he broke it and began to eat. They were all encouraged and ate some food themselves. Altogether there were 276 of us on board. When they had eaten as much as they wanted, they lightened the ship by throwing the grain into the sea.

When daylight came, they did not recognise the land, but they saw a bay with a sandy beach, where they decided to run the ship aground if they could ... In this way everyone reached land in safety.

Acts 27:9–39 and 44b

TO SET THE SCENE

Look at a short segment of the film The Perfect Storm.

It is remarkable that Paul trusted God throughout this storm, despite his own probable sea-sickness and the likelihood of death by drowning. His example challenges us to do the same, however hopeless our circumstances may seem.

WHAT DOES SEARCH THE BIBLE SAY?

1. Why was Paul on this ship at this time of the year? Look at Acts 23:11, 25:11–12, 26:32 – 27:1 and 12.

WHAT DOES SEARCH THE BIBLE SAY?

2. Compare this storm with the one that hit Jonah's boat in Jonah 1. Are there any similarities between the two storms and their outcomes? Does this tell you anything about the way God guides his servants?

HOW DOES THIS APPLY TO ME

3. Are you aware of any Christians you know who are facing storms or possible shipwreck in their faith, marriage, work or church? How about your own experiences, now or in the past? What encouragement is there to keep trusting God in the middle of it all in Paul's experiences of Acts 27?

4. Why do you think God allowed Paul to go through this experience?

5. How do you think Paul survived this storm that lasted for two weeks? What 'methods' do you think he used to preserve his own hope when others around him were abandoning theirs?

6. How did Paul witness for his faith during this difficult time? Look at verses 21–26 and 33–36 and list the ways in which Paul was a witness on that ship.

7. Look at verse 33–38. What were the effects of Paul's actions here? What do they tell you about Paul's blend of spirituality and common sense?

8. How does Paul's example of trust and enduring hope in this Bible passage make you feel about some of the situations you or others known to you are facing?

WORSHIP

▶ Sing *Faithful One, so unchanging* or listen to it on a CD, and thank God that 'All through the storm his love is the anchor'.

▶ List any whom you know to be facing storms or even shipwreck of their faith and pray for them, perhaps reviewing Question 3 above.

▶ Pray for one another as you face different storms and troubles.

DURING THE WEEK

Ask God to show you if someone you know is passing through a storm, and make a point of praying for them and doing something practical to show your love. Send them a card, or a small gift, or maybe plan to visit them.

FOR FURTHER STUDY

Look at Job 23:1–12 to see how Job trusted through the terrible storms he faced. He lost his children, his possessions and his health, and yet he continued to trust God. What does verse 12 tell you about the resources that Job drew upon to keep going?

Take a look also at some of the other tough situations that Paul faced in his ministry in 2 Corinthians 11:22–29 and prepare for next week's study of 2 Corinthians 12:7–10.

TRUST WHEN THE ANSWER IS NO

AIM

Aim: to discover how Paul trusted despite his thorn in the flesh

TO SET THE SCENE

Take a photocopied sheet of paper with the words P-R-O-U-D and H-U-M-B-L-E written downwards on the left hand side, and use each letter to suggest another word or phrase that describes the effects of pride or humility in our lives and communities: eg. P – polluting, R – rude, etc.

Read the passage together

I must go on boasting. Although there is nothing to be gained, I will go on to visions and revelations from the Lord. I know a man in Christ who fourteen years ago was caught up to the third heaven. Whether it was in the body or out of the body I do not know—God knows. And I know that this man—whether in the body or apart from the body I do not know, but God knows—was caught up to paradise. He heard inexpressible things, things that man is not permitted to tell. I will boast about a man like that, but I will not boast about myself, except about my weaknesses.

Even if I should choose to boast, I would not be a fool, because I would be speaking the truth. But I refrain, so no-one will think more of me than is warranted by what I do or say.

To keep me from becoming conceited because of these surpassingly great revelations, there was given me a thorn in my flesh, a messenger of Satan, to torment me. Three times I pleaded with the Lord to take it away from me. But he said to me, "My grace is sufficient for you, for my power is made perfect in weakness." Therefore I will boast all the more gladly about my weaknesses, so that Christ's power may rest on me. That is why, for Christ's sake, I delight in weaknesses, in insults, in hardships, in persecutions, in difficulties. For when I am weak, then I am strong.

2 Corinthians 12:1–10

2 Corinthians 10–13 has a different tone to the first nine chapters. Paul writes to defend his apostolic ministry from a minority in Corinth who claim that he is not really an apostle. A group he describes in verse 11 as 'super apostles' have questioned his credentials, and Paul is pressed by their slander into defending himself.

WHAT DOES THE BIBLE SAY?

1. Look at the list of Paul's sufferings during his ministry in 2 Corinthians 1:8–10 and 11:23–29. What is it about these passages that reveal Paul's true apostleship? Why do you think some at Corinth failed to understand this (See 11:7–9 and 12:13)? Could such misunderstanding occur today?

2. When it comes to visions and revelations Paul has quite an experience to recount. What should we learn from verse 6 about how to deal with spiritual experiences in general?

3. Look again at verses 7–10. Why did God allow Paul to have a thorn in the flesh? Why is spiritual conceit so dangerous?

> 'This statement is probably the most candid, transparent and vulnerable admission that any servant of Christ has ever made. Could you admit, because of your pride, that you actually need a thorn in the flesh? And yet it is the insecure person who will not talk like this. Many of us are far too proud to admit that we are full of pride!'[6]

4. Despite the fact that Paul knows that his thorn in the flesh is a messenger of Satan, he understands that God could remove it. What does that tell you about Paul's concept of the work of Satan? How do you think Paul coped with the news that his thorn in the flesh would not be taken away?

6 R T Kendall, *The thorn in the flesh* (London: Hodder & Stoughton, 1999) p5

HOW DOES THIS **APPLY TO ME** **5.** Have you had experiences where you have prayed very specifically for something, and received a totally unexpected answer? How did you react then, and would you react the same today?

WHAT DOES **THE BIBLE SAY?** **6.** Read Hebrews 12:5–11. We are told here to 'endure hardship as discipline' (v7). Why is discipline to be welcomed in a Christian's life? What is it for?

7. According to verses 8–10, what is the key to the power of Christ resting on Paul? How does this link up with the ministry of Jesus (2 Cor. 13:4)? Why?

WHAT DOES **THE BIBLE SAY?** **8.** Read 1 Kings 19:11–13. What do you think the Lord was trying to convey to Elijah by these displays? What do these verses show us about the nature of God and his power?

9. In 2 Corinthians 12:10 Paul does not say that when he is weak then the Lord is strong. He claims 'when I am weak, then I am strong'. How do you understand the difference?

Several Christian leaders have known great weakness... Charles Spurgeon had frequent periods of dark depression; Selwyn Hughes was bereaved of his wife and both his sons during his ministry; Rob Parsons and his wife Di have battled with ME in Di's life; Fanny Crosby, the great hymn-writer, was blind from birth; Joni Eareckson Tada is a quadriplegic; yet each has brought great blessing to the Christian church and beyond. 'When I am weak then I am strong.'

WORSHIP

Read Philippians 4:4–13. Thank God for Paul's ability to trust and to praise despite his thorn in the flesh.

Share with the group if you feel that you have a 'thorn in the flesh.' Pray for one another to be aware of what God is saying to you in your desire for him to take it away.

DURING THE WEEK

Find space to read Philippians 2:1–11 and think about the example of humility that Jesus set us. Pray that whatever you do might be done without 'selfish ambition or vain conceit' (v3). Pray for the leaders of your church that God will help them to remain Christ-like and humble in their service for the Lord.

FOR FURTHER STUDY

RT Kendall's book is a must for further study on the subject of Paul's thorn.

See also Joni's book *When God weeps* for an insight into what keeps her going despite her 'thorn in the flesh'.[7]

Psalm 139 offers a further insight into God's intimate knowledge of us and his gracious presence with us through all our trials.

---

7 Joni Eareckson Tada and Steven Estes, *When God weeps* (Grand Rapids: Zondervan, 1997).

TRUST COSTS

Aim: to understand that there may be a price to pay for trusting

TO SET THE SCENE

Have some finger food that represents areas of the world where Christians are being persecuted for their faith: China, India, the Middle East, Nigeria, Indonesia, Philippines – the choice is wide. Or imagine yourself being arrested and locked up in solitary confinement for a long period. You can only take one book of the Bible and one other book with you. What are they? Tell the group.

Read the passage together

And what more shall I say? I do not have time to tell about Gideon, Barak, Samson, Jephthah, David, Samuel and the prophets, who through faith conquered kingdoms, administered justice, and gained what was promised; who shut the mouths of lions, quenched the fury of the flames, and escaped the edge of the sword; whose weakness was turned to strength; and who became powerful in battle and routed foreign armies. Women received back their dead, raised to life again. Others were tortured and refused to be released, so that they might gain a better resurrection.

Some faced jeers and flogging, while still others were chained and put in prison. They were stoned; they were sawn in two; they were put to death by the sword. They went about in sheepskins and goatskins, destitute, persecuted and ill-treated—the world was not worthy of them. They wandered in deserts and mountains, and in caves and holes in the ground. These were all commended for their faith, yet none of them received what had been promised. God had planned something better for us so that only together with us would they be made perfect.

Therefore, since we are surrounded by such a great cloud of witnesses, let us throw off everything that hinders and the sin that so easily entangles, and let us run with perseverance the race marked out for us. Let us fix our eyes on Jesus, the author and perfecter of our faith, who for the joy set before him endured the cross, scorning its shame, and sat down at the right hand of the throne of

God. Consider him who endured such opposi-
tion from sinful men, so that you will not grow
weary and lose heart. In your struggle against
sin, you have not yet resisted to the point of
shedding your blood.

Hebrews 11:32 – 12:4

Hebrews chapter 11 is known as faith's hall of fame and lists many of the well-known heroes of the faith in the Old Testament. This last part includes some who did not have an easy experience of faith, but who just kept on trusting despite persecution.

1. What are the results of trusting God in verses 32–35a and how are they different from those listed in verses 35b–39?

2. What do Hebrews 11:1–2 and 39–40 teach us about the trust shown by all the people listed in 11:32–38, whatever their outcomes might have been?

3. In Hebrews 12:1 we read about 'such a great cloud of witnesses'. Who are they and what does this mean? What does the Christian race require of its participants?

WHAT DOES
SEARCH
THE BIBLE SAY?

4. Read Ephesians 2:8–10 to see how Jesus is both the 'author and perfecter of our faith' (Heb.12:2). How does 'fixing our eyes on him' help when we are being persecuted?

5. What effects should considering Christ's sufferings for us (Heb.12:3–4) have?

WHAT DOES
SEARCH
THE BIBLE SAY?

6. Read John 15:18–21, 16:1–4. What is the attitude of Jesus towards the opposition that Christians should expect? What reasons does he give for the persecution of believers?

HOW DOES THIS

APPLY TO ME

7. Read 1 Peter 4:12–19. Have you been insulted for the cause of the name of Christ? Are you aware of ways in which your personal or professional life has been adversely affected by your profession of faith in Christ? How did you feel about this?

> QUESTION: If you were arrested and charged with being a committed Christian, would there be enough evidence to convict you?

ENGAGING WITH

THE WORLD

8. What do 1 Peter 3:13–17 and 4:19 teach us about the way we should react to those who insult or persecute us for our faith?

APPLY THIS TO

MY CHURCH

9. Is your church engaged in any way with Christians who are suffering for their faith around the world? How could you be more involved?

10. It has been said that the blood of the martyrs is the seed of the church. Do you know of any situations where this has been the case?

> China became a Communist nation in 1949. ... In just one city in China, Wenzhou in Zhejiang Province, forty-nine pastors were sent to prison labour camps near the Russian border. Many were given sentences of up to twenty years for their "crimes" of preaching the gospel. Of those forty-nine pastors, just one returned home. Forty-eight died in prison. In Nanyang, believers were crucified on the walls of their churches for not denying Christ. Others were chained to vehicles and horses and dragged to their death.[8]

8 Brother Yun and Paul Hattaway, *The heavenly man* (London, Monarch, 2002) p20

WORSHIP

Read 2 Corinthians 10:3–4. The weapons we use to wage war are spiritual and prayer is one of the most effective. Look at some recent reports of the persecution of Christians for their faith drawn from Open Doors, www.opendoorsuk.org.uk or the Barnabas Trust www.barnabasfund.org . Pray about one or two of these difficult situations. Pray that the faith of those who are being attacked will remain strong.

DURING THE WEEK

Jesus said that we are to pray for those who persecute us or mistreat us. If there is anyone in those categories in your life, pray for them this week.

As you pray the Lord's Prayer, think seriously about the words 'as we forgive those who trespass against us' and how they apply to your own life.

FOR FURTHER STUDY

Read Matthew 25:34–40 and consider how Jesus wants us to react to the fact that so many Christians are in need. 1 Corinthians 12:24–26 also show the principle of our responsibility to other members of the body of Christ.

For a challenging and uplifting report on the state of the Christian church in China, one of the countries where the most intense persecution has taken place, see if you get hold of David Aikman's book *Jesus in Beijing*.[9]

9 David Aikman, *Jesus in Beijing* (Oxford: Monarch, 2005)

TRUST ALWAYS

AIM

Aim: to grow in confidence that we can trust God always

TO SET THE SCENE

▶ Have you ever bought a product on the basis of the reputation of the manufacturer alone? Were you happy or disappointed with the goods?

▶ Have you ever been given a personal promise or guarantee by someone you respect? How did you feel about that? Did they keep their word?

▶ Look at the adverts from some recent magazines. Which ones are based on the name and reputation of the manufacturer alone?

Read the passage together

I consider that our present sufferings are not worth comparing with the glory that will be revealed in us. The creation waits in eager expectation for the sons of God to be revealed. For the creation was subjected to frustration, not by its own choice, but by the will of the one who subjected it, in hope that the creation itself will be liberated from its bondage to decay and brought into the glorious freedom of the children of God. We know that the whole creation has been groaning as in the pains of childbirth right up to the present time. Not only so, but we ourselves, who have the first-fruits of the Spirit, groan inwardly as we wait eagerly for our adoption as sons, the redemption of our bodies. For in this hope we were saved. But hope that is seen is no hope at all. Who hopes for what he already has? But if we hope for what we do not yet have, we wait for it patiently. In the same way, the Spirit helps us in our weakness. We do not know what we ought to pray for, but the Spirit himself intercedes for us with groans that words cannot express. And he who searches our hearts knows the mind of the Spirit, because the Spirit intercedes for the saints in accordance with God's will. And we know that in all things God works for the good of those who love him, who have been called according to his purpose.

For those God foreknew he also predestined to be conformed to the likeness of his Son, that he might be the firstborn among many brothers. And those he predestined, he also called; those he called, he also justified; those he justified, he also glorified.

What, then, shall we say in response to this? If God is for us, who can be against us? He who did not spare his own Son, but gave him up for us all—how will he not also, along with him, graciously give us all things? Who will bring any charge against those whom God has chosen? It is God who justifies. Who is he that condemns? Christ Jesus, who died—more than that, who was raised to life—is at the right hand of God and is also interceding for us. Who shall separate us from the love of Christ? Shall trouble or hardship or persecution or famine or nakedness or danger or sword? As it is written: "For your sake we face death all day long; we are considered as sheep to be slaughtered." No, in all these things we are more than conquerors through him who loved us. For I am convinced that neither death nor life, neither angels nor demons, neither the present nor the future, nor any powers, neither height nor depth, nor anything else in all creation, will be able to separate us from the love of God that is in Christ Jesus our Lord.

Romans 8:18–39

THE PROBLEM OF SUFFERING

The problem of suffering is one of the questions at the root of all religions and human philosophy. Why we suffer, why life is so unfair, why bad things happen to good people – these are huge issues. There are no final answers to them, but in Romans 8 Paul asks us to consider the following:

▶ We serve a suffering Lord. Jesus has suffered terribly along with his created beings. Verse 17 speaks of sharing in his sufferings, before the next verse even looks at our own. We share in his sufferings:
  ▶ He did it all for us: see Isaiah 53:4,5.
  ▶ There is a cross at the centre of our faith. Jesus told us to take up our cross and follow him – there is a price to pay, a stigma for being a disciple.

▶ If we suffer with him, we shall reign with him! This is his promise to all who trust despite their sufferings.
▶ God can make all our sufferings count in the process of changing us to become more like Jesus.
▶ Nothing in creation can stop God loving us, now or in the future.

It is always easier to trust God when things are going well, but how about when we are 'groaning inwardly' or experiencing 'present sufferings'? Paul wrote this passage to help us to endure just such circumstances.

1. Read verse 18 again and also 2 Corinthians 4:16–18. What are the keys in these verses to hope that endures despite our present sufferings?

WHAT DOES SEARCH THE BIBLE SAY?

2. Read Romans 5:1–5 and 1 Peter 1:6–7. What produces hope in the Christian's life?

3. What signs do you see that 'the whole of creation is groaning as in the pains of childbirth' (v22)? What do you think this means?

4. What aspect of enduring hope does Paul comment on in verses 24–25?

5. According to verses 26–27, what is the role of the Holy Spirit in our prayers?

6. Verse 28 is possibly one of the best known verses in the New Testament. What do you understand by the phrase 'all things'? In the light of verse 29, what kind of good do you think God has in mind for those who love him?

> 'God is more concerned with conforming me to the likeness of his Son than leaving me in my comfort zones.' Joni Eareckson Tada [10]

WHAT DOES SEARCH THE BIBLE SAY?

7. Read Psalm 56:9 and Romans 8:31. How did David know that God was for him? How do we know that God is for us? What are the implications of this for us?

10 Joni Eareckson Tada, *When God Weeps* (Grand Rapids: Zondervan, 1997) p121

> 'While God is for us, and we keep in his love, we may with holy boldness defy all the powers of darkness.' – Matthew Henry

WHAT DOES **SEARCH** THE BIBLE SAY? **8.** Read Romans 8:1–4 and verse 34. Why is there no condemnation for Christians?

HOW DOES THIS **9.** How does the knowledge that God does not condemn you make you feel? Is it any easier to trust in the light of this? If APPLY TO ME so, why?

10. Read verses 38–39 again. Why should the Christian not be afraid of anything at all in all of creation, either now or in the future?

HOW DOES THIS **11.** Do you find it easy to trust those who love you? God could not do any more to demonstrate his love for you than he has APPLY TO ME done in Christ. How does that make you feel?

> 'There may actually be times when trust is just about all we can bring as an offering to God. Times of pain and struggle, when we've come to the end of ourselves and feel like we have nothing left to give. In these moments to say to God "I trust You" can be an offering pleasing enough in and of itself. ... we are telling God that despite our circumstances, we still believe He is who He says He is. And God loves that kind of heart response.'[11]

---

11 Matt and Beth Redman, *Blessed be Your Name* (London, Hodder & Stoughton, 2005) p85

WORSHIP

Read Romans 8:28–39 in one of the more recent paraphrases such as *The Message* or *New Living Bible*. Spend a few moments thanking God for his amazing love.

Read Psalm 56:8 – 57:3 out loud as a group (NIV). If you are finding it hard to say 'in God I trust' (v11), then ask someone in the group to pray for you.

DURING THE WEEK

Look again at the list of Paul's own suffering in 2 Corinthians 11:22–29 and reflect on what Paul meant when he said that 'in all things God works for the good of those who love him'. How do you think he sustained this level of trust?

If you are aware of a member of the group who has struggled with these studies because of their own circumstances, plan to be in touch with them this week to encourage them, either by a visit or telephone call.

FOR FURTHER STUDY

Read Zechariah 3:1–7 for an Old Testament example of God dealing with the accusations of Satan and declaring his servant Joshua clean (the High Priest not the successor of Moses).

1 John 4:4 and Hebrews 13:6 continue this theme of trusting God to take away our condemnation and give us boldness to serve him in all circumstances.

LEADERS' GUIDE

TO HELP YOU LEAD

You may have led a group many times before or this may be your first time. Here is some advice on how to lead these studies:

▶ As a group leader, you don't have to be an expert or a lecturer. You are there to facilitate the learning of the group members – helping them to discover for themselves the wisdom in God's word. You should not be doing most of the talking or dishing out the answers, whatever the group expects of you!

▶ You do need to be aware of the group's dynamics, however. People can be quite quick to label themselves and each other in a group situation. One person might be seen as the expert, another the moaner who always has something to complain about. One person may be labelled as quiet and not be expected to contribute; another person may always jump in with something to say. Be aware of the different types of individuals in the group, but don't allow the labels to stick. You may need to encourage those who find it hard to get a word in, and quieten down those who always have something to say. Talk to members between sessions to find out how they feel about the group.

▶ The sessions are planned to try to engage every member in actively learning. Of course you cannot force anyone to take part if they don't want to, but it won't be too easy to be a spectator. Activities that ask everyone to write something down, or to talk in twos and then report back to the group, are there for a reason. They give everyone space to think and form their opinion, even if not everyone voices it out loud.

▶ Do adapt the sessions for your group as you feel is appropriate. Some groups may know each other very well and will be prepared to talk at a deep level. New groups may take a bit of time to get to know each other before making themselves vulnerable, but encourage members to share their lives with each other.

▶ Encourage a number of replies to each question. The study is not about finding a single right answer, but about sharing experiences and thoughts in order to find out how to apply the Bible to people's lives. When brainstorming, don't be too quick to evaluate the contributions. Write everything down and then have a look to see which suggestions are worth keeping.

▶ Similarly encourage everyone to ask questions, to voice doubts and to discuss difficulties. Some parts of the Bible are hard to understand. Sometimes the Christian faith throws up paradoxes. Painful things happen to us that make it difficult to see what God is doing. A housegroup should be a safe place to express all this. If discussion doesn't resolve the issue, send everyone away to pray about it, and ask you minister for advice!

▶ Give yourself time in the week to read through the Bible passage and the questions. Read the Leaders' notes for the session, as different ways of presenting the questions are sometimes suggested. However, during the session, don't be too quick to come in with the answer – sometimes we need space to think.

▶ Delegate as much as you like! The easiest activities to delegate are reading the text and the worship suggestions, but there are other ways to involve the group members. Giving people responsibility can help them own the session much more.

▶ Pray for group members by name, that God would meet with them during the week. Pray for the group session that it will be a constructive and helpful time. Ask the Lord to equip you as you lead the group.

THE STRUCTURE OF EACH SESSION

Feedback: find out what people remember from the previous session and if they have been able to act during the week on what was discussed last time.

To set the scene: an activity or a question to get everyone thinking about the subject to be studied.

Bible reading: it's important actually to read the passage you are studying during the session. Ask someone to prepare this in advance or go around the group reading a verse or two each. But don't assume everyone will be happy to read out loud.

Questions and activities: these are designed to promote discussion on how to apply what the passage says to your individual/group situation.

During the week: a specific task to do during the week to help people put into practice what they have learned.

Prayer: suggestions for creative prayer. Use these suggestions alongside other group expressions of worship such as singing. Add a prayer time with opportunities to pray for group members and their families and friends.

GROUND RULES

How do people know what is expected of them during your meetings? Is it ever discussed, or do they just pick up clues from each other? You may find it helpful to discuss some ground rules for the house group at the start of this course, even if your group has been going a long time. This also gives you an opportunity to talk about how you, as the leader, see the group. Ask everyone to think about what they want to get out of the course. How do they want the group to work? What values do they want to be part of the group's experience: honesty, respect, confidentiality?

How do they want their contributions to be treated? You could ask everyone to write down three ground rules on slips of paper and put them in a bowl. Pass the bowl around the group. Each person takes out a rule and reads it, and someone collates the list. Discuss the ground rules that have been suggested and come up with a top five. This method enables everyone to contribute fairly anonymously. Alternatively, if your group are all quite vocal, have a straight discussion about it!

ICONS

 The aim of the session

 Engaging with the world

 Investigate what else the Bible says

 How does this apply to me?

 What about my church?

NB – not all questions in each session are covered, some are self-explanatory.

SESSION 1

MATERIALS REQUIRED

You will need some small slips of paper for the forgiveness part of the worship time if you feel it is right to go that way, and the CD *Home again* volume 4, VMD8044R Vineyard Music, Track 7 (*Only You*).

TO SET THE SCENE

The answer is, of course, that the surgeon is not the patient's father because she is his mother! The time it takes for people to realise this reveals how much we have stereotyped brain surgeons as men. Things are not always as we imagine them to be. Joseph was an ex-slave with a history of rejection in his childhood who was imprisoned for alleged sexual offences, but he was not your stereotypical prisoner.

1. Clearly jealousy is a major factor here, though your group may find others. A discussion about sibling rivalry may also follow.

2. Reuben may well have felt a special sense of responsibility as the first-born, but he was not strong enough in his convictions to overturn the decision made by the others.

3. Joseph clearly maintained his trust in God and his relationship with God despite all the rejection he had suffered, and his enslavement. For a similar attitude, see the account of Naaman's maid in 2 Kings 5:2–3. Like Joseph, this little Israelite girl managed to overcome her understandable bitterness to be a witness in her captivity and bring blessing to her captors.

4. Joseph has not lost his desire to be a witness for the God of Israel, despite his desperate circumstances. His integrity shows up in the trust he was given by the prison warden, and the fact that anything Joseph was responsible for did not need the warden's own supervision. Joseph's trust in God is also evident in his desire to give God the credit for being with him, and for interpreting dreams (40:8b).

5. This and 6 will be a very important part of the study as you invite group members to consider their own witness and reputation with outsiders. It may be wise to sub-divide the group down into smaller units to discuss these questions.

6. Try to avoid too deep a discussion here on the sovereignty of God but rather focus on the way that God over-ruled the wickedness of the brothers to bring about his own purpose for Joseph and, even more significantly, for Israel.

7. Here is a wonderful opportunity to explore the place of forgiveness in the process of trusting God when betrayed. The signs of Joseph's forgiveness included the fact that he urged them not to be afraid of him, he reassured them and spoke only kindly to them, and he made practical provision for their needs and those of their families.

8. This question and the worship that follows must be approached with real care. Pray for wisdom to know how to lead the group in an act of forgiveness.

WORSHIP
The reading from the Psalm will help to keep your eyes on the main theme − trusting when rejected by others − but your group members may well become focused on the need to forgive. That's fine because in order to trust following rejection or betrayal, we do need to forgive, but it would be good to refocus on the theme before you close. The song will help you to do that.

Some may find it helpful to write down the names of those they need to forgive and, following prayer, to destroy the piece of paper, possibly burning it as a sign of their resolve.

SESSION 2

TO SET THE SCENE

The first activity can be played like a game of consequences. Write the name of a group member at the top of a long slip of paper, one for each member of the group. Invite the group to pass these around so that everyone has to write down a positive comment about the person named at the top of the paper, and then fold it over and pass it on, so that at the end each person will receive their own paper back with several comments underneath it.

1. The impact of the frequent invasions from the desert was enormous. The people of Israel were largely farmers at that time, and found that the incoming hordes of heavily armed and brutal nomads were overwhelming. Look at verse 2 and verse 6 in particular.

2. The point here is that Gideon was threshing wheat in a winepress. Normally this would have been done in an open or hilltop area giving plenty of breeze. Here he is working in an enclosed winepress because of his fear. At least there are the early signs of slight resistance to the enemy occupation in his decision not to allow the Midianites to get hold of his grain.

3. Both Gideon and Mary have difficulty in seeing themselves from God's point of view. Their self-doubt is fairly obvious. Gideon begins with a frank exposé of his doubts about God's presence with him.

4. Gideon argued that God must have abandoned Israel because they had been invaded and over-run by the Midianites, yet the unnamed prophet had already warned Israel that this is the consequence of their disobedience to God (v9), as had Joshua (Josh. 23:15–16) many years before. God had not abandoned Israel. He was giving them the consequences of their choices in judgement, in order to bring them to repentance.

5. Gideon, like Moses, felt unworthy to fulfil God's call, and pointed to his low birth, and the low social standing of his family. In fact, the evidence of verses 30–32 suggests that Gideon's father was well respected in the town, so Gideon was underestimating himself and his family. We are often quick to run ourselves down but that is not how God sees us, and often not the way others see us either.

6. The words used by the Lord in both cases were a solemn promise that God would be with them. This overcomes our sense of low value or ability, for the God of all the earth is with us. See Psalm 46 and Romans 8:38–39.

7. There will be differing responses to this according to the experiences of your group members.

8. Gideon trusted God and his word enough to go and start trying to change things in the religious life of his community. He acted on his trust, not on his fears, although his actions were tinted by some measure of fear (v27) revealing a very touching humanity and room to grow in Gideon's faith.

9. This may well have been some of the 'room to grow' in Gideon's faith. God honoured Gideon's requests, and he may graciously honour ours, but there are other ways of guidance set out in Scripture (prayer, the word of God, the counsel of wise friends and leaders, inner peace etc). If we accept Gideon's fleece as a template for contemporary guidance, we may be inconsistent. He had several wives and a concubine, and was a brutal killer too (Judg. 8:21, 29–31) but we certainly do not recommend such behaviour today.

WORSHIP

Ask some members of the group to look up Bible verses that spell out God's attitude of love towards us, and have them read them out loud. Here are some:

Psalm 100:3; Isaiah 40:11; Jeremiah 29:11–13; 31:3; Luke 12:32; John 15:9; Galatians 2:20; Hebrews 13:5–6;

Gideon's trust was shown in his willingness to obey despite his fear and his low sense of self-esteem. Listen to the song *Have your way* in me (*Home again*, volume 4, track 4) and ask your group to let God have His way in their lives, no matter what they may feel about themselves.

SESSION 3

TO SET THE SCENE

Listen to the CD track 5 *Come now is the time to worship*. You may already have it, but if not you will find it on CD *Home again* volume 4, VMD8044R Vineyard Music.

1. Job's losses were total. He faced bankruptcy because his flocks and herds were his savings, investments, capital and stocks. He also lost his sons and daughters so that his dynasty was at an end, along with any hope that he might receive dowry for his daughters.

2. There are signs of Job's robust trust in God in the reading, and also in the first chapter. He shows the key trait (also seen in Joseph) of integrity. Taken from the little Hebrew word *tam*, it means 'whole, sound, complete, entire, unimpaired and healthy'. Also Job 1:5 shows that Job had a real horror of the sin of cursing God, and recognised that it could even be committed in the heart, if not openly, when we don't like what God is doing in our lives. Most remarkable of all, he had come to the place of willingness to accept bad things as being from God as well as good.

3. God is proud of Job's obedience and faith and holds him up before Satan as an example of the very righteousness that Satan hates and wants to destroy. God trusted Job to be able to cope with the trials that he allowed Satan to inflict.

> 'God has faith in his people. It is a risky position for the Almighty to take and here he entrusts his reputation to a man: 'Have you considered my servant Job?'[12]

4. Satan, meaning the accuser, is given leave to test Job, but his power is on a leash (2 Cor. 12:7, Heb. 2:14–15). This is not a battle between equals. God is in charge, and Satan may only go so far and no further. We are, at present, in the period of the 'now and not yet' of the Kingdom of God, but the day will come when Satan and his angels will be totally destroyed.

5. Allow the members of the group to share their own experience of pain and suffering here, and acknowledge the reality of the struggle to accept bad things as from the hand of God. Jesus shows us the way, though, in Gethsemane, where he faced the cross, knowing that it was what fitted into the saving purposes of a loving Father.

12 Dennis Lennon, *Encounter with God in Job* (London: SU, 1995) p18

6. This is remarkable trust because it is resting on a living Redeemer at such an early stage of the life of Israel. It also displays a confidence in the after-life and the resurrection of the body which is way ahead of its time.

7. It was a persevering trust – it didn't give up. Also, he chose to trust in God, not in himself. Job 23:10 could be paraphrased 'I don't know what's going on but he does, so I am going to trust that when this is through, I will be a better person for it.' See James 5:10–11. Job's trust was also an obedient trust, as he walked through his life carefully following God's ways (Job 23:11). It was also a trust in God's word, which he treasured more than his food (Job 23:12).

8. Try to avoid negativity here, but invite honesty.

9–10. Worship in times of pain and suffering is an immense challenge for Christians. Job is our example. In these circumstances worship becomes the 'sacrifice of praise being the fruit of our lips' from Hebrews 13:15. Even in the darkest situation, however, we have an enduring hope in God who is our Redeemer. Worship focuses our attention on the Lord instead on our pain. Worship draws us closer the heart of God who is the source of strength and peace in trouble.

SESSION 4

1. The disciples were in the position they were because Jesus had told them to go. They were being obedient to the Lord, and might have expected an easier time. An opposing strong wind meant that it was all hands to the oars, and conditions were bad. Jesus was up the mountain in prayer. John 6:14–15 show that he needed some space following the miracle of feeding the five thousand.

2. Despite his need of rest, and the fact that he was in prayer, Jesus kept an eye open for his disciples. When you take into account that it was dark and stormy, between 3am and 6am, and that they were at least three miles away, it is remarkable that he was aware of their needs. Look at Matthew 28:18–20 and consider that whenever Jesus sends his people out on a mission, his promised presence is with them.

3. The issue here is fear. Both fear of the unknown and fear of the supernatural were quite understandable given the circumstances, but Jesus addresses those fears with his command 'Take courage, it is I. Don't be afraid.' There are 366 times that the Bible says 'Fear not' – one for every day of the year and one more for a leap year!

4. It will be important not to be judgemental during this part of the study, and to avoid the temptation to try and fix anything that might be revealed. People may just need the loving space to express their fears, even if they include some fear of the work of the Holy Spirit. What these disciples presumed was a ghost turned out to be the Lord, but it will be best to avoid being drawn in to ghosts and spooks here.

5. What may be reflected in these other accounts is a degree of embarrassment among the other disciples that they did not trust the Lord in quite the same way as Peter did. The fact that Peter (if he did direct Mark) omitted it himself may just be a sign of his own reluctance to boast. There are lessons for us as we consider how to handle spiritual experiences when it comes to sharing with others.

6. Peter did not limit his idea of what might be possible to what he had experienced in the past, or what others might think is possible. A survey of the disciples' opinions would never have produced the outcome. God was going to do something new, something unique to Peter's own experience. Peter knew that nobody can walk on water. Yet it is no surprise that, if Jesus is who he says he is, that he can both walk on water and cause Peter to do so. We must not limit God. Peter also heard the call of Jesus and decided to step out in obedience. He

left the comfort zone of the boat where all the others were content to stay, and set off on a risky walk of faith.

7. If the whole group are from the same church, this may allow for a more in-depth discussion about risk, taking in the context of the church's life. If they are not, it may be better to focus on the experience of the group members themselves.

8. Peter did actually walk on the water. That should not be overlooked in the light of what happened next. He began to sink when he 'saw the wind' probably referring to the boisterous nature of the sea around him. His fisherman's logic kicked in and he was afraid again. He had taken his eyes off Jesus to look at his surroundings and realised that, naturally speaking, he should not be doing what he was doing. When he realised he was sinking, he did the right thing. He refocused on Jesus and cried out 'Lord, save me.' We need to keep our eyes on Jesus (Heb. 12:2).

9. The rebuke is actually quite a mild one, and one that simply recognises the facts. The term 'little faith' can refer to a tiny fledgling bird that is still developing, so you might translate the words of Jesus as 'O you of fledgling faith' and then it becomes clearer. Little faith is still of value in the teachings of Jesus (see Lk. 17:6).

10. This is an opportunity to list some of the points above: Peter's willingness to take a risk, his lack of concern about what others might think, his desire to hear and to obey the command of the Lord, his ability to turn back to the Lord quickly when sinking and his humble cry in his moment of need.

WORSHIP

As people share whatever they may feel God is calling them to do as a step of faith, ask group members to pray for them. If someone shares an idea that sounds totally off the wall and causes you concern, offer to discuss that with them privately after the group has ended.

Watch out for those who say nothing and encourage them to be open to the possibility that God is also calling them to follow him in simple and challenging steps of obedience. Encourage the group to remember one another during the week, and perhaps to hold one another accountable for some of the steps of faith shared.

SESSION 5

MATERIALS NEEDED

The cd that you will need for the Worship section is CD *Home Again* volume 4, VMD8044R Vineyard Music, Track 6 (*Faithful One*).

Also, get hold of *The Perfect Storm* starring George Clooney before the group meeting and check it through to find the scene that in your opinion gives the most dramatic and lifelike portrayal of a storm at sea. Have a look at either the dramatic and true account of the rescue of the crew of the yacht Mistral, or else the scene where the anchor breaks loose on the Lady Grey and George Clooney has to climb out on a limb of rigging to fix it. *The Perfect Storm* is available on video VHS and DVD, and also scenes can be downloaded from http://perfectstorm.warnerbros.com/cmp/splash-fr.html

1. It would be good as background reading and preparation for you to trace the pattern of events that led up to this storm from the arrest of Paul in Jerusalem in Acts 21:27, through his appearance before the Sanhedrin in Acts 23, his transfer to Caesarea under Roman protection in the same chapter, his trials before Felix and Agrippa and his appeal to Caesar. This led to him being on the ship as a prisoner on his way to Rome.

2. There are similarities between the storms of Jonah 1 and Acts 27 – get your group to list them. The lesson is that God does use adverse circumstances to guide his servants, either in rebellion (as in the case of Jonah) or in obedience (with Paul).

3. It will be possible to pray for the folk who may be mentioned here a little later, but if you feel it more appropriate to pray for them now, do so. It would not be helpful to spend too long on this.

4. It is amazing that Paul was on board at all. Having been given divine orders to go to Rome, you would imagine that the way would be plain sailing. But it was not. Nor was there any sign of Jesus walking on the waters to deliver them. Things are not always just as we would like them to be when we are obeying God. Some of the answers here include: because he wanted the gospel to be sent to Malta, because he wanted a witness on a boatful of people who were facing death, because he wanted Paul to grow in faith through facing adversity on his way to Rome and because God felt compassion for the father of the Roman governor of Malta who was desperately ill.

5. Here are just some ideas:
   ▶ He was a prisoner, but not a victim. Paul was a prisoner on this ship, but he acted at times as if he was the captain (v31). When we face storms we do not need to be victims. It is all about attitude. It matters how we perceive ourselves in the storm.
   ▶ He looked for God's perspective on his situation. Things are not always as they seem. It's clear that whilst others were panicking, or shoring up the ship, Paul was seeking the Lord (vv23–26).
   ▶ He reminded himself of who he was in Christ. See verse 23, 'Whose I am and whom I serve' – Paul knew who he was in Christ.
   ▶ He chose to believe what God had said more than his immediate circumstances. He had no evidence for what he told the crew other than what he had heard from the Lord (v25). His faith was not in faith, nor in man, but in the word of the Lord.

6. Paul gave a very strong witness for the Lord on the ship. He did so by clearly giving warnings to both the crew and his fellow passengers on what would be the outcome of their actions and choices, (vv10 and 31). He also witnessed by maintaining a positive approach throughout. He was constantly encouraging others (v36). He would not enter into despair. In addition, as a step of faith, he gave thanks to God for his food in front of all of them (v35). Even the simple act of taking food was a sign of hope.

7. Verses 33–38 show us that Paul was aware of God but also intensely practical. He trusted God but he also warned them that they had to eat something in order to survive (v34). This balance of spirituality and sound common sense is so important.

8. This may lead to lively debate in which there is probably no right or wrong answer, but gives the chance to air different views.

9. Without dominating the group, there may be an opportunity for you to show an example here by an honest account of how you have trusted God (or otherwise!) during some stormy time.

WORSHIP

If your group are not singers, or you have no musician, you may prefer to the CD of this great worship song. This CD is especially designed for small groups and may prove useful on other occasions during this series.

Ask the group for the privilege of being able to pray with them if they are passing through terrible storms in their own experience right now. Encourage members of the group to pray for each other.

SESSION 6

MATERIALS NEEDED

You will need to make, in advance, a photocopied sheet of A4 for each group member with the words P-R-O-U-D and H-U-M-B-L-E written downwards on the left hand side.

TO SET THE SCENE

The exercise is designed to let your group be creative with words as well as introducing our subject. Once the sheets are completed, ask the group for synonyms for the words based on each letter (you may need to consult a dictionary or Thesaurus in advance!)

1. Paul's willingness to trust God and remain in service despite all these hardships is evidence of his calling and apostleship. He also feels the weight of genuine concern for the churches (11:28−29) in contrast to his accusers who seem to be more interested in the financial support of the churches (11:7−9, 12:13). The believers in Corinth had been seduced into thinking that prosperity and ease were signs of spiritual authority. This is a danger in certain sections of today's church, where prosperity and abundance are again seen as signs of God's approval.

2. Paul asks to be judged by what he does and says and not by any special visions or revelations that he may have been granted. These are still the benchmarks for assessing Christian maturity. Our conduct and speech, not charismatic gifts or spiritual experiences, are the indicators of character − the true mark of spiritual maturity.

3. Paul is quite clear that it was to prevent him from becoming conceited. Kendall also suggests that it was a 'chastening' from God, a manifestation of God's glory and a means of sanctification.[13] As to what Paul's thorn may have been, there are many theories and possibilities (Kendall claims to have heard over fifty!) Galatians 4:12−16 has led some to suggest an eye condition, malaria or epilepsy as the culprit. It is significant that it is not made clear in the New Testament, which means that Paul's thorn may be representative of any condition, mental, marital, spiritual or physical, which keeps us humble and dependent upon God's grace.

4. Similarly to the lessons learnt from the book of Job, we see Satan portrayed here as subservient to the will of God. This 'messenger of Satan' seems to be fulfilling God's intention to overcome the danger of conceit in Paul. If God

13 Kendall, 7−20.

wished, he could simply remove the thorn. Instead, God's grace is offered as a means of coping with Satan's messenger. Remarkably, Paul seems able to turn from pleading for its removal in verse 8 to delighting in it in verse10. This is not masochism but rather an example of the power of God's grace.

5. This will give the group members an opportunity to share their own disappointments when it comes to prayer. Care should be taken to avoid offering slick answers as to why this might have been.

6. Discipline for the Christian is a sign that God is treating us as his children. It is for our own good, and also a way for us to share in his holiness. It is never pleasant, but can bring about a harvest of righteousness and peace in our lives in the long run.

7. It appears that being able to 'boast about weakness' (rather than about our strengths) and delight in difficulties is a key to the power of Christ resting on Paul. The reasoning in 2 Corinthians 13:4 is that Paul is the servant of a crucified Saviour, so weakness (as seen at the cross) is at the heart of the gospel.

8. In this classic Old Testament passage we have a display of God's power in front of the discouraged Elijah. He might have expected God to speak 'through the earthquake, wind and fire' but God chose instead to reveal himself in a gentle whisper. This reinforces Paul's understanding of the nature of God's dealings with his people. God can speak through weakness and gentleness as well as in the storm, or through works of power. Indeed, he may even prefer to do so.

9. It always seems so much easier to confess that when we are weak, God is still strong. After all, he never changes, does he? But for us to acknowledge that we actually become stronger when we are weak is much more a statement of trust. It is a mystery – yet it was foundational to Paul's ministry and effectiveness as an apostle.

WORSHIP

The reading and prayer time should reinforce Paul's attitude of trust in God, even though his desperate pleadings were not answered in the way he would have liked. Ask for permission to pray with anyone who expresses a sense of struggling with a 'thorn in the flesh' in their own discipleship.

SESSION 7

1. The results of trusting God in verses 32–35a were in keeping with the previous part of chapter 11, showing great outcomes, victories and deliverances for those who trusted God. Verses 35b–39 show a different group of believers who did not receive the answers they hoped for. They chose to endure, hoping instead for a better resurrection. They suffered the most appalling privations and were given the commendation that the world was not worthy of them.

2. The words 'commended for their faith' serve as book ends for this chapter's review of what it means to trust God. The fact that they were all commended equally means that the faith of those who were not delivered from their enemies, or who wandered around in deserts or hid in caves, was of the same value to God as those who received some sort of miraculous breakthrough. The statement that 'only together with us would they be made perfect' means that for both them and us the fulfilment of God's promises is found in Jesus.

3. The word translated witness here is the root of our English word martyr and means those who testify at great personal cost to what God has done for them. The image in these verses is of an athletics contest in a stadium, where the runners are being cheered on, not just by spectators but by those who have run the race before and proved God's faithfulness to them and theirs to him. Those who run the Christian race must do so with perseverance when the going gets tough, and also by letting go of anything that would hold them back.

4. In Ephesians 2:8 we see that faith is the gift of God, making him its 'author'. His perfecting of our faith is illustrated in verse 10 where we are seen as God's workmanship, doing those good works in Christ that he has prepared in advance for us to do. This teaches us that God's grace and kindness are the source of our ability to trust in him. Jesus is also the Author of our faith, in that he is the perfect model of one who trusted despite the personal cost.

5. Considering Christ's sufferings should help us not to grow weary and lose heart. It can be a good antidote to self-pity when we are having a difficult time living for Christ in the face of opposition, as none of us has suffered like Jesus did. He is also able to draw close to us when we do suffer: he knows what it feels to keep trusting despite persecution.

6. Jesus foretells that Christians will be hated by those who hate him and all he stands for. As servants of Christ we should expect this and not be shocked. Christians do not 'belong to the world' but have been chosen out of it. This can make us a target for persecution, but should not make us so strange that we

lose our ability to speak effectively to people who do not share our point of view. Jesus also foretold religious persecution where those who kill Christians will do so thinking they are serving God. This was fulfilled in the New Testament by Jewish persecution, but has its equal today in religious fundamentalism of all kinds.

7. 1 Peter 3:13–17 tells us to maintain our Christian witness in such circumstances with 'gentleness and respect' and to avoid wrongdoing so that our behaviour may speak for itself in the face of malicious slander. 1 Peter 4:19 goes even further, urging suffering believers to commit themselves to God and to continue to do good.

8. There are many reports of remarkable church growth in nations where early pioneers of the faith were martyred, such as Mozambique, Korea, China and India. Aikman believes that the number of Christians in China today is close to eighty million, despite the continuing persecution of the churches, particularly the house church movement.

If you do not have access to the Internet, further information on the persecuted church can be obtained from:

Open Doors UK	*or*	**The Barnabas Fund**
P.O.Box 6		The Old Rectory
WITNEY		River Street
Oxon		PEWSEY
OX29 6WG		Wilts
		SN9 5D

SESSION 8

MATERIALS

You will need a range of magazines or newspapers that contain adverts that make use of the manufacturer's name or logo very prominently in order to sell their goods. This is often the case with car makers or perfume producers.

1. We need to keep our eyes on the eternal dimension of our sufferings and remember that God has planned a glorious future for us, far better than where we are at the moment.

2. Having peace with God through the grace he has given us in Christ gives us hope. Also, suffering produces perseverance which in turn leads to the development of character in which hope is a part. The real source of Christian hope, though, is that God's love has been poured into our hearts by the Holy Spirit whom he has given us.

3. When the Lord Jesus does come again, he is going to transform everything that is upon earth. Until then, the after-effects of the fall of man are being seen in the planet. In Genesis 3:17 God said to Adam, 'Cursed is the ground because of you.' These words may be a prophecy of the environmental impact of man's sin and selfishness. This is another reason why there is so much suffering: global warming leading to floods, hurricanes, and even famine in some parts of the world. We live in a fallen world which itself is groaning with the weight of its fallen state, longing for the second coming of Christ. That groaning will increase towards the time of the Lord's return (Mt. 24:7).

4. Paul comments on the invisible nature of the thing hoped for in these verses. As with faith, you only need hope when you have not yet got whatever you are hoping for.

5. Just as hope sustains the believer in suffering, so the Holy Spirit sustains our prayer lives. In verse 22 the creation groans, in verse 23 the believer groans, but in verse 26 the Holy Spirit groans. God shares in our distress. The Holy Spirit is so near to the heart of the Lord that he communicates without necessarily being audible.

6. This phrase is hard to understand. God works in all things for our good, even the evil things. 'The Spirit makes all things, even though they are evil, work together for good' – Martin Luther. This does not make God guilty of the evil. We live in a corrupt world, and man is responsible for his own actions and sins. Yet, in all things, God by his transcending power is able to make circumstances

serve our ultimate good. See Genesis 50:19–21. Also, God's aim is clearly set out in Romans 8:29, for us 'to be conformed to the likeness of his Son.' He is working on our character to make us more like Jesus, whilst we are most often concerned with our desires. He sees everything from the vantage point of eternity and knows what is truly best. When we look at a tapestry, say the famous Bayeux tapestry that depicts the battle of Hastings, from the wrong side, we can only see the tangled threads and a mess of colours. Looking on the right side shows us the beauty of the pattern and design. When we reach heaven we shall look back and see the real story of the battle of life.

7. David knew that God was for him when his enemies suddenly turned back and fled. We know that God is for us because of Calvary – God did not spare his only Son but gave him up for our sakes. This means that we should not be afraid of what people may say of us or to us, or even do to us, because God is with us in life's struggles.

8. Condemnation is dealt with through the death and resurrection of Jesus. If there is any doubt about this, Paul says that now Christ is interceding for us at the right hand of God.

9. God's persevering and unconditional love is the key to dealing with our fear. There is nothing at all that we can do, or in all of creation, that can make God love us any less, or indeed any more, than he does already.

The worship will give an opportunity for you to sum up much of what this course has been about. Trusting in the darkness of our suffering is tough, but as we have seen, it is possible with God's help. Pray with those who share that they struggle to trust and ask God to fill them with the knowledge of his love through the Holy Spirit.